THE FUTURE
BODY LAN

How to communicate effectively in business through multimedia

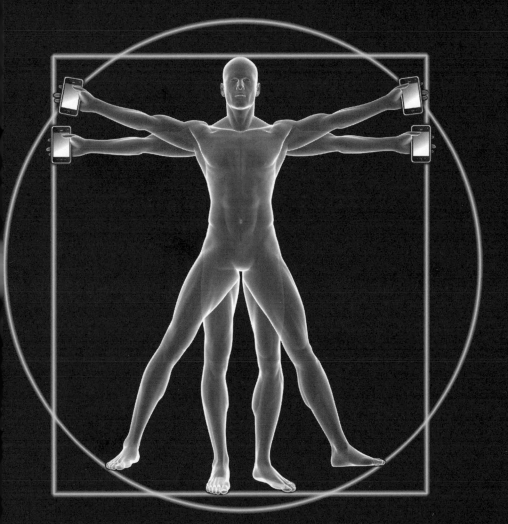

Carole Railton

The Future of Body Language
How to communicate effectively in business through multimedia

©Carole Railton

ISBN: 978-1906316-62-4

Published in 2011 by HotHive Books, Evesham, UK.
www.thehothive.com

The right of Carole Railton to be identified as the author of this work has been asserted by her in accordance with the Copyright, Designs and Patents Act 1988.

A CIP record of this book is available from the British Library.

Printed in the UK by TJ International, Padstow.

'It's a great time
to be alive because this is
the generation that gets to
change everything.'

Paul Hawken, environmentalist and author

CONTENTS

7   Acknowledgements

9   Foreword

11 About the author

15 Introduction

19 Chapter One – Face-to-face communication

41 Chapter Two – The telephone

55 Chapter Three – Email, text and social networking

65 Chapter Four – Webcasts and YouTube

75 Chapter Five – Skype and video conferencing

87 Conclusion

93 What people say about Carole Railton

ACKNOWLEDGEMENTS

ACKNOWLEDGEMENTS

This book exists because of the team around me, for which I am extremely grateful.

In particular, I would like to thank Tricia Ward, who saved my mind when I had to reduce the book to the size it is now; Sara Drinkwater, my editor; and Karen Swinden, my publisher. Between them, they captured my ideas, focused my attention and helped the book arrive safely.

I also thank Robynne Fletcher and Sarah Kent for their encouragement, and all the people who have already read the book or contributed with their references, including Steve Westall, Keith Francis, Bibi Lynch, Moira Taylor, Adrian Ramsey, Lisa White, Nicola Dennes, Andrea Wilson, Tom Evans, Robin Freeman, Mark Underwood, Allan Pease, Andrew Cuthbert, Will Broom and Bruce Lloyd, and others along the way who have encouraged and supported me.

Most of all I would like to thank you, the reader, for taking the time and effort to read this little book.

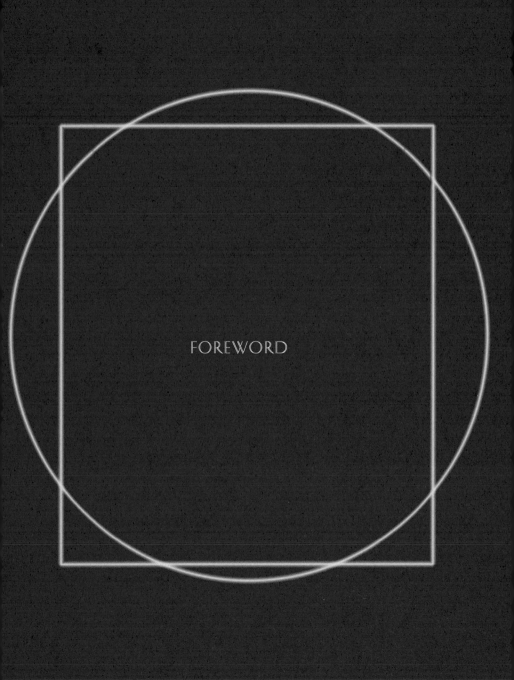

FOREWORD

When we look back on this time in history, we will realise that we were part of a cultural shift. Online communication and the tools that make it possible are having a profound impact on society. This book serves this shift and it is critical for people to absorb and act on the information it contains.

Carole Railton is determined to make her mark on the individuals that are living through this change. Many focus on the technology and forget that it is only there to serve. People are at the end of the keyboard as you type, and recognising the impact your words and 'language' have on others could make the difference between survival and starvation in the future.

In a time when businesses are seeking to be more efficient, both in terms of time and money, this book is a valuable tool to help individuals understand each other and get their messages across as succinctly and effectively as possible. With this in mind, the book provides a series of bite-sized exercises to teach key skills. These include improving your posture so that your messages are clear and free of mixed signals, developing an authoritative voice tone to help you get the most out of telephone communications, and learning breathing exercises to calm your nerves before doing live presentations, whether on stage or screen.

In addition, the book tackles common business issues such as how to deal with telephone rage, how to prepare for a presentation, how to compose effective emails and how to manage multiple conversations on Skype. This book draws attention to the impact of non-verbal messages and will empower readers by equipping them with vital tools to get the most out of their communications. We are now part of a connected world, far beyond the traditional skills and role models we held in the past. Learning how to communicate online is essential and I am delighted that a book like this is available from someone who clearly has the experience and sensitivity to teach it.

ABOUT THE AUTHOR

ABOUT THE AUTHOR

For the past 10 years Carole Railton has been carrying out ground-breaking work as a behaviourist, specialising in body language and using her skills to help people maximise their potential, both socially and in the world of business.

Originally a high flyer in the business world, Carole worked for Rank Xerox for 10 years – first in sales, then as a training manager and finally as manager of sales operations in nine Middle Eastern countries.

Then she set up her own consultancy, livingsuccess.co.uk, to help individuals develop their understanding of who they are and how they can influence others.

Then came lifeafterbranding.com, for companies who want their staff to have better relationships internally and with the organisations and clients they work with. These projects have been so successful that she now works with another personal brander in the States to offer the best of both worlds.

Carole has in-depth knowledge of many different cultures. She has worked in 47 countries as an employee and a consultant, including the United States, South Africa, the Middle East and the UK, and has travelled to many more in search of insights into how people interact.

This global perspective makes this book essential reading for anyone wanting to establish contact with people around the world.

Her experience in all tiers of business – from sales, recruitment and training to management for companies including IBM and Datapoint – makes this an invaluable tool for people working in all areas of business.

Along the way, Carole has collected qualifications in many areas (Neuro Linguistic Programming, homeopathy, coaching for business and directive breathing). She is a Fellow of The Royal Society of Arts, and a member of the Wise Women Network and of XLN, an organisation that promotes the elimination of poverty worldwide.

She lives in central London, but travels extensively – giving talks, delivering workshops, making radio appearances and writing for women's magazines.

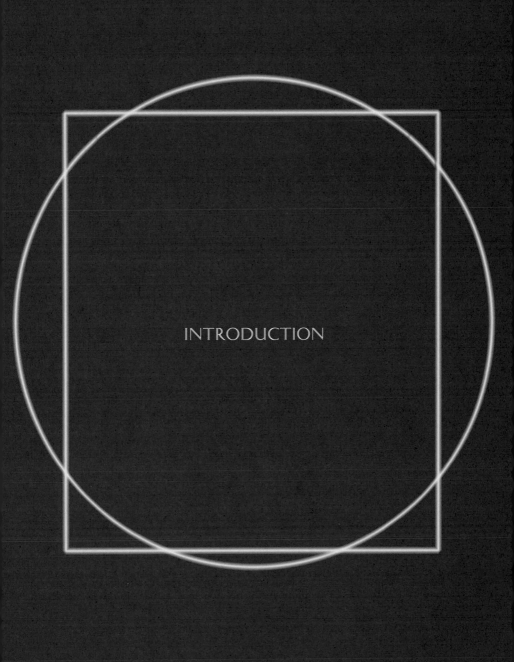

INTRODUCTION

INTRODUCTION

The aim of this book is to equip readers with the right body language skills to deal with any business situation that involves communicating through modern technologies such as Skype, podcasts and video conferencing. The book will offer fresh observations and insights into how you can adapt your own body language when using these technologies so that you present yourself in the best possible way.

Research carried out by Albert Mehrabian in 1971 has shown that when we communicate with people, 57% of that communication is visual, 36% is related to tone and 7% takes the form of spoken words. Originally, most of our communication with business people was held face to face, through networking events and meetings. This meant that we were able to take full advantage of all three elements of body language to get the most out of our interactions.

The first technology to revolutionise business communication was the telephone, in 1876. This meant that face-to-face meetings were no longer essential, which had a great impact on body language. By removing the visual element of communication this made the importance of our tone of voice and spoken words even greater.

With increasing speed, more and more technologies have revolutionised business and the way we communicate. The 1980s and 1990s saw the introduction of email and the internet, which left just 7% of our communication skills open for interpretation. More recently, the introduction of video conferencing, Skype and websites such as YouTube has brought the visual element of body language back into play in the business world, as people hold more and more face-to-face meetings online and use web videos to promote themselves and their companies.

Technology has now taken us full circle, with all three aspects of body language instrumental in our communication skills once again. This means that businesses can communicate more quickly and effectively; however, if individuals aren't using the right body language skills for each technology then they will experience the reverse effect.

The introduction of these technologies has had a massive impact on the generations born after the second world war, resulting in the baby boomers (born between 1946 and 1964), Generation X (born between 1965 and 1981) and Generation Y (born 1982 onwards). It is worth considering how such changes in technology affect these age groups.

Traditionally, because baby boomers were born during the age of face-to-face meetings, they have very good visual communication skills and, on the whole, are good at reading body language. Generation X has excellent written communication skills and is great at email and telephone communication, while Generation Y prefers instant messaging, podcasting and texting as communication tools. This book will look at these communication methods, and in the conclusion will go on to provide some tips for each generation to get the most out of their communication skills.

It is a widely held belief that Generation Y is most familiar with technology, and therefore will adapt best to any advances in this area. However, with the increasing use of podcasts (audio) and video (visual) across the web, the focus is back to visual and verbal communication. Hence it is likely that, with a bit of practice, all three age groups can make excellent use of advancing technology.

Are you ready to start taking active steps to significantly enhance your communication skills? Then let's get started.

Carole

It is important to remember that body language skills aren't about seeking to influence people; they are about openness and sharing so that both parties get the most out of the conversation. It is also important to remember that the focus should not be on just one aspect of body language, but the whole situation in context.

A common example of this is the misconception that folded arms always indicate someone is angry and defensive. In fact, many creative people have their arms folded for inspiration, as they are subconsciously forcing thoughts up through their body. Therefore, when considering body language skills, ensure you do so at all times with an open mind.

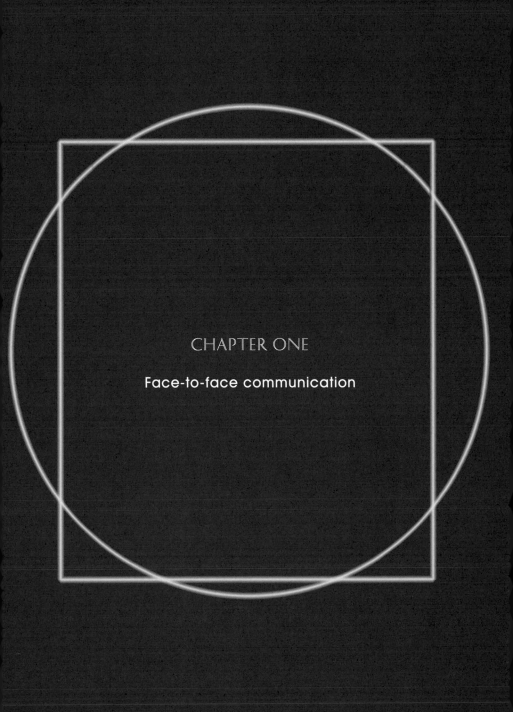

CHAPTER ONE

Face-to-face communication

CHAPTER ONE
Face-to-face communication

As we discussed in the introduction to this book, when you meet with someone face to face you have the advantage of being able to use all three aspects of body language – visuals, tone and words.

Before we look in detail at the impact of technology on our body language, we need to look at face-to-face communication and the key elements involved.

According to University of Toledo psychology professor, Dr Frank Bernieri, we make up our minds about someone within the first 30 seconds of meeting them. We then reinforce this belief based on whatever they do in the next few minutes. For example, if we decide that we dislike a person and then a few minutes later they drop their papers on the floor, this compounds our dislike as we see them as clumsy and untidy. Had we decided we liked them, by dropping their papers they would have seemed to confirm to us that they are simply human and make mistakes just as we do.

This makes it even more important that we make the right first impression, as it will be very difficult to change people's minds about us if we don't. In this chapter we will look at the three areas of body language and discover how to make sure yours is giving the best possible impression.

There are many ways in which we can categorise people. As well as separating them into baby boomers, and generations X and Y, it is also possible to categorise people according to their personality types. It is helpful to understand people and the types of body language that members of each group will be sending out, in order to be able to relate to them. We know of course that each of us is different, but it pays to understand the rough categories we can all be placed into so that we can make more informed decisions about how to work with different people.

There are a number of ways of doing this, predominantly using psychometric testing. The diagram below demonstrates the four different profiles which I have put together using Dr Tony Alessandra's *The Platinum Rule* and my training at Xerox:

Organised/Pragmatic/Fast Moving	
Typical occupations	This person can be found running an organisation – they tend to be directors and entrepreneurs.
Speed of movement	You will notice they both move and talk quite quickly.
Use of body language	They use minimal body language unless they feel under pressure, in which case they may increase the amount of movement to get their point across.
Use of language	They will often talk about the bottom line: people of this type are concerned about their company's goals and identifying the strategy necessary to achieve them.

Extrovert/Leading/Excitable	
Typical occupations	This person often takes sales jobs or jobs where they are required to influence others.
Speed of movement	They are fast, generally enticing others to follow.
Use of body language	They make use of body language in most of their communications.
Use of language	Since this group of people like excitement and drama they are likely to choose and use words that create drama and action.

Analytical/Researching/Steady	
Typical occupations	These people are usually scientists, IT gurus, engineers, accountants and auditors.
Speed of movement	They are generally paced, not fast.
Use of body language	This is often the most-disguised body language user. They internalise their world and don't tend to look outwards, so their body language expressions are more subtle.
Use of language	People in this group take a questioning stance and are always striving for detail; they want to know how things work.

Amiable/Seeking Structure/Like To Please	
Typical occupations	This group includes nurses, carers, arbitrators and counsellors – people who are able to empathise.
Speed of movement	They are slow – patient and considered.
Use of body language	They keep opinions to themselves so their body language tends to be more hidden, making it easy to misread.
Use of language	This is the person who finds it difficult to say no. If you ask them a direct question, they are likely to say yes just to keep the peace.

This table demonstrates that if you are working with someone who is highly analytical you will need to be the most open you can, as they are the most secretive. This might mean having your palms showing and legs uncrossed, demonstrating typical open behaviour, making it easier for them to communicate with you.

On the other hand, if you are dealing with someone you believe is pragmatic then you should make your communications short, direct and to the point, as this person has an organised time schedule and dislikes detail. Your body language will need to be clean and support your talk, because generally this is the person that can read body language without too much training.

Meanwhile, if you are speaking to an extrovert they are likely to give all their feelings away in their voice and body movements, which are typically fast and dramatic. The easiest thing to do here is to mimic them and feed back their words to them, so you are exciting them too! By contrast, amiable people will need a very comforting response from you, so use gentle body movement and voice tone to communicate with them most effectively.

As we continue through the book, dealing with the different technologies and the body language we demonstrate when using them, we will consider these personality types and how to deal with them.

There are also some inherent differences between body language as used by men and women that are useful to remember. Men tend to remain much stiller when talking and presenting, while women move around much more. When I am running a training course I will always demonstrate this point by asking a female to come into the room and get the participants to count her body language movements as she circles a table. I then ask a man to come in and do the same. In every case the woman performs more movements.

This creates the impression of men having more authority, as stillness suggests composure, but in fact often doesn't indicate this at all. It is simply the way women naturally present themselves. If you are a woman it is helpful to be aware of this and make a conscious effort to stand still when talking to others, particularly men, as this will help to bridge the gap between you.

Men also tend to sit with their legs open or stand with their legs apart, which creates the impression of balance and openness. This pose feels very unnatural to women, who tend to keep their legs together and often cross them when sitting down. When communicating with others these natural body language poses need to be taken into consideration so that wrong impressions are avoided.

At all times it is important to remember to be yourself. You shouldn't try to fit into a mould, or be what you think others expect you to be, as this will not work. If you want to build a lasting relationship with another person you need to be open and honest so they are working with the real you. It is impossible to help develop someone who always puts on a front.

Visual

The visual aspect of body language covers everything that you notice about a person's appearance, including their mannerisms and posture. This is the area that most baby boomers excel at, while it is widely felt that people in the X and Y generations need to hone these skills.

Face

The first thing you are likely to notice about someone when you meet them is their face, so it helps you to connect with them quickly if you understand more about what their face reveals. Face reading is a practical skill that can be utilised by all. It allows you to enhance business dealings and fulfil your potential. Just imagine what you could do at a first meeting if you had an idea of what others were like and how they preferred to take in information. The ability to influence proceedings would also increase your confidence.

Over the page are four common types of faces and details of what can be learnt from them.

These are general examples, and I caution you to read this book thoroughly so that you can couple the information you read in the faces of others with the rest of their body language to get an accurate representation of the person.

FACE SHAPE	WHAT THIS SAYS ABOUT MEN	WHAT THIS SAYS ABOUT WOMEN
Round	He will have a calm approach to life.	She is logical, caring and open, and thinks in the long term.
Oval	He has a sense of justice and makes a good manager or diplomat.	She will be confident, steady and reassuring. Women of this face shape are often teachers, leaders and models.
Square	He will be interested in influencing others.	She will like good quality, is powerful and has high demands.
Long	He is logical and pragmatic, and thinks things through.	She is powerful and will take action, generally using logic to get what she wants.

Knowing that people are likely to fall into one of the above categories will help you better understand those you approach. It is also useful to work out which of these types best describes you, so that you can ensure in networking situations that you gravitate towards like-minded people.

There are in fact more face shapes than shown above, but this selection is included to demonstrate the most prominent. If you have an interest in face reading I recommend you read a copy of Naomi Tickle's *You Can Read a Face Like a Book* to explore the subject further.

Posture

Posture is the foundation of body language; we make our minds up about people based on how they present themselves, making good posture one of the most important skills you will learn.

Think for a moment of the two extremes of bad posture. At one end you may think of a tramp, someone whose shoulders are very slumped over and whose head is facing the ground, making him look victimised and unapproachable.

At the other end of the scale is a bouncer – someone who has a protruding chest, with broad shoulders and his head held high, making him look powerful, but, again, unapproachable. As most people want to look friendly and encouraging to others, we need to position ourselves somewhere in the middle. The ideal posture to hold is one of a straight back, with your head balanced centrally on the spine; being symmetrical gives confidence. Try the exercise below to see what your posture is saying about you:

> > > E X E R C I S E < < <

- Sitting or standing in front of a mirror with both feet firmly on the ground, breathe naturally and quietly observe the following:

- Is your head pulling forward on your neck? If so, this is a sign that you strain, either to look at the computer screen or to get yourself noticed. Generally people who walk with a pronounced projection of the head forward are 'head led', they are cerebral folk and are likely to fall into the analytical category that we discussed in the introduction.

- Is your head pulling backwards from your neck? If so, this can indicate a fear of getting involved, which is common in an amiable person.

- With both these positions, work to gently re-centre your head over your spine, shoulders dropped to a natural relaxed position and pulled slightly backwards, which will open up your chest area and aid circulation and relaxation.

- Is your head leaning to one side? When your head leans to the left or right it could be an indicator of how you use equipment – your phone, for example. Again, move your head to the centre of the top of your spine for a more comfortable position.

Because we have spent years misusing our bodies it pays to do this exercise daily, observing and shifting back to centre. Over time not only will you look and feel better, you will begin to have more success in your life as your body adopts the pose of composure.

Breathing

Breath is the biggest indicator of someone's feelings, so you will be able to tell a lot about someone just by the breaths they are taking. Short breaths from the top of the chest indicate the person is stressed or anxious, while deep breaths from the bottom of the stomach suggest the person is relaxed and comfortable.

If you struggle to pick up on how someone is breathing then try watching their shoulders. A very relaxed person who is breathing from their lower body will hardly be moving their shoulders, while someone who is feeling anxious will be moving their shoulders quite rapidly.

When you first meet someone and want to interact with them, it is important to watch their breath pattern and then mimic it to help put them at ease. If their breathing is particularly shallow you can help reduce their nerves by mimicking their shallow breaths and gradually bringing them round to deeper, more controlled breathing without them even realising it.

Eyes

Everybody knows that eye contact is important when communicating with others, and most people are also aware that it is considered rude to stare. Therefore, where the eyes are concerned, the most important part of body language is to really understand how to use them.

We can tell a lot from looking at someone's eyes. Notice the space between the eyes of the person you are talking to – could you fit a third eye in there?

People with lots of space between their eyes tend to be more relaxed and see the bigger picture, whereas people with less space are likely to need detail before they can make a decision.

People with eyes set close together often find themselves in analytical jobs as a result, while those with a large space between their eyes are likely to be amiable and in jobs that make us all feel better, such as nurses, carers and counsellors.

The eyes are described as 'the window of the soul' and they certainly do give a lot away. Next time you are on a train or plane or in a lift, look someone in the eyes (be cautious here, don't get in a fight after they ask what you're looking at!). See if you can work out some information about them: what kind of job they have, their thought processes, their educational level or anything else. You will make amazing deductions based on just their eyes. Then look at the rest of their body language and their words to validate your initial impression.

Your left eye is considered as the receiving eye and your right eye is thought to be the giving eye; therefore when making eye contact with someone you should look into their left eye. This is seen as a gesture that is open and friendly, while not being overpowering. The other person will naturally and instinctively respond by looking into your left eye as well, which then puts you both on an even footing.

When you are in communication with anyone face to face, you are aiming for at least an exchange of information and ideally a satisfactory outcome. The quicker the information can be assimilated, the easier it is to complete your communication. We can do this by playing to their left side, the receiving side.

Previously, teachers of body language have suggested that you look at the triangle of the face, the nose and eyes. I firmly believe this is too strong a view to take of the person opposite you. A much easier stance for both of you while exchanging verbal information is to look into each other's left eye.

Using eye contact successfully will help you to achieve the results you want. This isn't about bullying people into seeing things as you do, but simply about persuading them to listen to your opinions and value them as much as they do their own. Try this exercise next time you want your partner or a friend to listen to you and see if you get better results:

> > > E X E R C I S E < < <

Start talking to your friend or partner looking into both of their eyes (staring). Then move to just looking into their left eye. You could even ask them after you have finished your conversation at what stage they felt at ease. It will undoubtedly be when you changed your gaze to their left eye.

This is an excellent technique for sales people as it helps your clients feel more relaxed about you. The aim here is for both of you to be looking into each other's left eye to speed things up. If you are an amiable person this is also a good exercise to practise because it will open you up and give you confidence to look someone in the eye without staring.

Our eyes are also indicators of our thought processes. When we are creating thoughts, images and feelings we will look to the right, and when we are remembering them, we will look to the left.

Looking up and to the right is about creating a visual image, and looking up and to the left corresponds with remembering one. Ask one of your friends to think about a green giraffe and watch their gaze flicker up and to the right.

When we look to the right without moving our eyes either up or down it is sounds and words that we are creating, and while doing the same on the left we are remembering them. When we look down and to the right we are creating feelings and emotions, and, to the left, remembering them.

Studies by Richard Bandler (the co-founder of Neuro Linguistic Programming) have shown that 90% of the population follow these rules. The diagram below summarises this information.

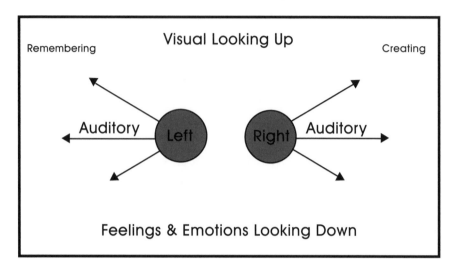

Test it out with your friends, as it needs quite a bit of concentration before you will be able to notice these clues and still keep talking! But when you master it, you will soon be able to understand how to interact with people more successfully. If they look up a lot it may help to switch to visual phrases, such as 'it looks like', 'I can see what you mean', or 'let me paint a picture for you'; or, if they look down a lot, phrases that correspond with feelings – for example, 'I get a feel for what you are saying'. If they are looking from side to side then they respond best to auditory phrases such as 'I hear what you are saying', or 'it sounds to me like...'. This way, you make it much easier for the other person to tune into what you have to say.

It is also helpful to notice other body language when speaking to someone face to face, and not to base your perceptions only on the fact that they are making eye contact. It is easy to believe that, because someone is looking at you, they must be interested in what you have to say, but you should also look at their feet to confirm this. If you see that their feet are actually pointing away from you this indicates that they would rather leave the conversation and be somewhere else.

What you do in this situation depends on the circumstances. If you are in an unexpected meeting with the boss or a client, then their body language indicates that this is not a good time for them and that you should make another appointment to see them.

If the meeting is planned then their body language indicates that they are perhaps not as confident with you as they could be, so you may need to work with them to address some underlying issues.

If you are at a networking event, then this is a signal that it is time to move on and speak to someone else, as there probably isn't any more to be gained from the conversation you are currently having.

Handshake

Usually when we meet someone our first physical contact is a handshake. Much has been printed about the importance of a firm handshake, but when it comes to body language what is more important is to make sure you use your handshake to open communication between you both.

To do this, make sure that when you walk towards the person you move slightly to the left of them, causing them to angle their body towards you. At this stage your feet are best positioned pointing towards them as this indicates that you would like to engage with them. If their feet are mirroring yours then you are both on an even footing and ready to start the meeting. If they are not, then this is a warning sign that they are distracted and you will need to try and engage with them as the meeting progresses.

Always look someone in the eye when shaking their hand as this gives confidence and security to the other person and they believe that you care.

Height

Height is important for visual communication, as people tend to look up to tall people. We bow down to people who are more senior than ourselves, such as royalty, and we also consider the penthouse to indicate luxury as it can be found at the top of the building. This means that shorter people may have to work harder in face-to-face situations. The following exercise will help you to make the most of your height:

> > > E X E R C I S E < < <

- Stand tall, with your head up and acknowledge yourself for who you are. Think of all the good things about you, every single one of them – really indulge yourself so that you become sure of yourself.

- The energy from this will spill out and people will feel that you are a wonderful person and treat you accordingly. This will make up for any difference in height.

Tone

Once you have had your initial encounter and placed yourself on an even footing with the person you are meeting, the next step is to start speaking to them.

As we already know, what you say counts for only 7% of their impression of you, while your tone of voice will count for 36%, making it well worth spending some time on. We are now going to look at some of the factors that affect the tone of your voice.

As with the impression you create visually, your tone of voice is strongly influenced by your posture. Try the following short exercise as an example:

> > > E X E R C I S E < < <

- Crouch over in your seat with your head nearly touching your knees and say 'good morning' out loud. Notice how your voice sounds.

- Now say 'good morning' while sitting up straight and notice how much brighter and sharper it sounds.

- Now say 'good morning' again, this time with your head tilted slightly back. Notice how much more your voice projects from this position.

If you look down, you restrict your vocal chords, making it impossible to have a strong voice (not to mention the poor visual impression you give!).

In many university lecture halls, theatres and auditoriums, the seats rise upwards from the stage in order to make the speaker lift their head to project their voice. Make sure you are doing the same.

As well as taking care not to restrict your voice by hunching, it is also very important to keep a centred posture so that your voice sounds balanced.

Maintaining good posture without slouching shows that we are not a pushover to others and that we are in possession of our own power. The more we practise good posture, the more good posture becomes the norm and we become healthier, happier and more positive.

When people have confidence in themselves or their authority they make less movement of the body; they gain authority by being still and clear in their body language. One of the quickest ways for you to demonstrate that you are clear in your communications is to have both feet on the ground.

The exercise below will demonstrate the importance of a balanced posture to the sound of your voice:

> > > E X E R C I S E < < <

- Work with someone else so you both see the difference this makes, or find a way of recording what you are saying while doing this exercise.

- Stand or sit with one leg on the floor. Start talking, or engage in conversation for about a minute, then put your other leg down on the ground so that both feet touch the ground. Notice what happens to your voice and your authority.

- If you are working with someone else, swap roles so you can observe.

Remember to have both feet on the floor when you want to appear clear, calm and authoritative.

How your health affects your voice

Your general health and stress levels will also be apparent in the tone of your voice, so it is important to ensure you look after yourself so you always sound at your best. Worry and fear have dramatic influence over our lives and when we aren't on top form it is pretty easy for others to detect this.

It is often difficult to do anything about being unwell, so if you really aren't looking and sounding well then it is a good idea to reschedule important meetings until you are feeling better. However, there is something you can do to help with high stress levels.

The following exercise is a quick way for you to change your body language and help ease your worries. This is a good exercise to do every morning when you arrive at work to simply clear your mind, or to use as a stress-buster whenever you are worried or concerned.

> > > E X E R C I S E < < <

- Firstly, stand up.

- Now look down at the floor and think your worst thought about the day ahead; what might happen, how bad could it get? Keep looking at the floor until you get a signal from your body. If things are really bad it might be a shiver, or it could be just complete absorption in the problem and a feeling of total desperation.

- Do this for at least two minutes, in your mind making the problem as big as you can.

- When you have achieved this, with both feet firmly on the floor, turn your head up so that your mouth faces the ceiling and your neck is dropped back.

- Now, think about the same problem again. Really focus while in this position, concentrating your mind on the same problems as before. Again do this for a minimum of two minutes.

- Relax your mouth, part your lips slightly and, when you can, force yourself into a huge smile.

A negative thought will have less impact if you look up than if you look down. You will feel that you can cope or that you know what to do, or you will have let go of the problem, and your body language will have returned to normal. In the unlikely event things didn't change, you simply need to take longer doing both parts of the exercise.

As well as changing your body language, this exercise also allows you to focus on what is good rather than what is bad, and, of course, doing this enhances your body language for the better. After all, who wants to be around someone who is worried, or afraid, or unhappy? It's much easier to be with someone who can cope, who is grateful for things and who projects good energy.

How your personality affects your voice (negativity vs positivity)

It is understandable that your take on the world will influence how your voice sounds. A generally pessimistic person will have a dull voice, while a generally optimistic person will have a brighter, chirpier voice.

It is important to remember that a key aspect of body language is to be yourself. Society needs both optimists and pessimists in the world; for example, an analytical person, such as a medical researcher, needs to keep questioning their discoveries and seeing the downsides of the drugs they are developing, or they wouldn't do such a great job. However, it is important to try and keep pessimistic tones out of your voice in order to progress your relationships with others.

On the other hand, pragmatists and extroverts tend to use their voices to dominate and may need to talk more gently to allow others to have a voice.

The difference between male and female voices

The epiglottis, a small valve of cartilage at the base of the tongue, is responsible for the changes in the tone of your voice and vibrates differently for men and women.

Your size, your sex and the way you pass air through the voice box cause vibrations in the auditory system and the force of air affects the tone and volume of the voice.

It is well known that men and women have voices that are differently pitched – men tend to have lower voices, which often sound authoritative, while women are usually more softly spoken.

In this day and age when equality is paramount, women need to be more assertive with their voices to ensure they are on an equal footing with men.

An exercise to improve the authority in your voice is available in Chapter 2 on page 46. Men, on the other hand, may need to tone down their voice when speaking to avoid sounding aggressive.

The throat is a delicate organ that needs to be taken great care of and used properly. This involves avoiding screaming too often and remembering to give your voice a rest if you are starting to lose it or are hoarse for any reason. Continually straining your voice can have a permanent detrimental effect.

Although words only count for 7% of communication, they are still worth some consideration. There are a few words that are best avoided if you want to come across as confident, assured and open:

WORD TO AVOID	REASON	ALTERNATIVES
should	This word implies that you think you are better than other people and have the authority to tell them what to do.	could
why	This word sounds blaming, untrusting and interrogative.	how
try	This word sounds non-committal.	yes, no, will

Below are the key face-to-face body language skills you should now be aware of:

- It is helpful to understand the four general personality types people can be categorised as in order to get the most out of communication with them.
- There are some inherent differences between the natural body laguage of men and women that it is useful to be aware of.
- A key aspect of body language is to be yourself.
- There are four general face shapes – you will benefit from having a basic understanding of what this can tell you about a person. It is also helpful to identify what face shape you are.

- We make our minds up about people by how they present themselves – posture is very important.
- Breath is the biggest indicator of someone's feelings, so you will be able to tell a lot about someone just by the breaths they are taking.
- When making eye contact with someone you should look into their left eye.
- Our eyes are indicators of our thought processes – if you can master this you will find it easier to tune in to people.
- Make sure you use your handshake to open communication between you and the person you are meeting.
- People judge you by their perception of your level of authority, so the more authoritative you can make your voice sound the better.
- If you look down you are restricting your vocal chords, making it impossible to have a strong voice.
- Remember to have both feet on the floor when you want to appear clear, calm and authoritative.
- There are a few words that are best avoided if you want to come across as confident, assured and open.

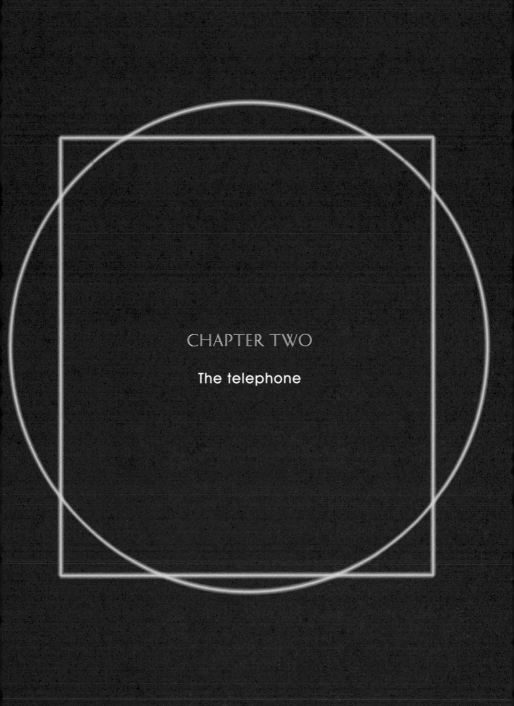

CHAPTER TWO

The telephone

CHAPTER TWO
The telephone

When the first telephone was invented, it was a tremendous novelty, but it has now evolved to become an everyday means of communication – the baby boomers and Generation X use it to make phone calls, while Generation Y use the text messaging facilities available on mobile phones.

The telephone also meant voice-to-voice communication was instant, and gave us the opportunity to talk to people across the world that we didn't know, in places that we hadn't visited.

The speed and the efficiency of the telephone was a great boon to social situations and to the expansion of businesses and markets across the world.

However, making the transition to speaking with others without actually being able to see them was not easy, as we all like to see who we are talking to. The ability to look at somebody face to face while talking to them seems far more natural; we can look them in the eye and get a sense of their reactions to us. We can make more judgements based on body language, some of which is subliminal, some obvious and some subtle.

Therefore, having lost 57% of your ability to communicate when using the telephone, you will find that tone and the words you use become increasingly important.

We often forget that our body language can affect our tone, but don't assume that, because the person you are speaking to can't see you your tone of voice won't be affected by what you are doing.

In this chapter we will look at some of the behaviours that have an impact on the tone of your voice.

How you are feeling

As discussed in Chapter 1, if you are having a bad day, if you are stressed, or if something has upset you then this will come out in your voice.

We may all be sitting in the same office, but what we see, hear and feel, and how that translates into body language, is different for everyone; we are truly all unique. If you are a pragmatist or extrovert you are more likely to reveal your emotions in your voice, while analytical and amiable personality types are more contained.

To make your business life easier, here is an exercise that will clear your mind and help you feel more positive and relaxed – giving your mind and body a chance to prepare before your busy working day.

Often we bring problems from home into work, and this has a disastrous effect on how we manage our day. So, before you start work on the telephone, here is what to do:

> > > E X E R C I S E < < <

- This will take about four or five minutes in total.

- Sit down, close your eyes, and breathe firmly and as far down into your stomach as you can.

- Now imagine that you have a large, open, empty black plastic bag floating just above you. Start to think about all the things that are not OK in your life right now; it might be words you have just heard, situations you are in, people you don't like, money problems, the target you have not reached, relationship issues – whatever the problem, drop them one by one into the open black bag. Keep going until you have exhausted all your issues.

- Make sure everything is in the bag and tie it up. Now let this heavy bag float up into the air and disappear, and as it does, it takes all your troubles and worries with it.

- At first some of you might find you can't generate a good visual image. This is OK because, when you keep practising this exercise daily, it becomes easier to visualise the black bag and also to perform the exercise in less time, so it's well worth the effort.

You need to sound bright and alert on the telephone, as the caller has nothing else on which to base their opinion but the tone of your voice and the words you are saying.

In most situations something as simple as a smile can make all the difference. Smiling affects the chemistry in your body; you are more likely to be healthy if you are happy.

Smiling can change our mood, the next time you are stressed put on a smile and your mood will change for the better.

People know when you are not smiling, and as most of us like to be around smiling and happy people, it makes sense to use your smile as often as you can in business. Successful people are more relaxed, have more fun and smile more.

Over the page is an exercise that helps you to think about smiling and alter your habits. Hopefully you will enjoy the fun of trying it, too.

- Screw your face up in an angry pose as tight as you can. Now speak, trying to sound happy and balanced while keeping your faced screwed up. It is absolutely impossible.

- Now, bring a broad smile to your face (you may need to think of a recent event that really made you laugh). With this smile on your face, talk and think as though you are very angry. Again, it's absolutely impossible to do this.

Sounding authoritative

It is important to be aware that people judge you by their perception of your degree of authority, so the more authoritative you can make your voice sound the better – particularly in the case of women, who often get mistaken for lower-ranking employees such as receptionists even if they are actually quite high up in their company.

Generally, people who have a lower tone to their voice are seen as senior, so master this aspect of voice and you can elevate yourself to a leadership position. And you do not need to be the boss to be the leader – anyone can step up to the challenge of leadership.

In order to achieve this and to sound assured, you need to have good posture and an open attitude. With pragmatists this is likely to be less of an issue as they are naturally more self-assured and decisive.

The exercise below will help other personality types to balance their tone of voice:

> > > E X E R C I S E < < <

- To start, place both feet on the ground, ensuring you are breathing from your diaphragm (this gives you stability and inner strength).

- Next, gently place your hands onto the desk or table in front of you, palms down and a shoulder width apart. A lighter method of doing this is to place your hands in the same way on top of your thighs instead of the desk. This will have the effect of setting your voice in your body. It becomes rounder and, by using your hands in this way, you encourage people to focus on you. The tone in your voice will now be knowledgeable and authoritative.

- When you want to re-introduce others to the meeting or conversation, remove your hands from the desk to encourage them.

Making a call

It is easier to make sure you sound authoritative when you are making a telephone call than in some other situations as you have time to prepare. You can ensure you have all your notes in front of you, and that your posture and breathing are appropriate for the call.

Back in Chapter 1 on page 33 we looked at how your tone of voice is affected by your posture. Let's take this one step further now with the exercise over the page:

- Crouch over in your seat with your head nearly touching your knees and say 'good morning' out loud. Notice how your voice sounds.

- Now say 'good morning' while sitting up straight and notice how much brighter and sharper it sounds.

- Now say 'good morning' again, this time with your head tilted slightly back. Notice how much more your voice projects from this position.

- Now repeat the three positions above and say the same words, but with the thought in your mind that you are very late for an extremely important meeting: perhaps a job interview, a presentation, or an appearance in court.

You will now have heard six different sounds from your voice, all within the space of one minute. This is evidence, if it were needed, that you really have to pay attention to what you are doing and how you are doing it whenever you are communicating with others over the telephone.

Radio presenters generally speak more slowly than the rest of us, take longer breaths and make sure their intonation is clearer. This makes for easier listening and also helps us feel more relaxed as we listen to them. While talking on the telephone it is very important to breathe evenly. Prior to making an important call, take two or three deep breaths and focus on what you are going to say and what you wish the outcome to be. When we take deep breaths we relax and concentrate better on the task in hand.

It is often more difficult to control your body language when receiving a call, as you may not be ready for it and also have no idea who is on the other end of the line.

However, if you find yourself in the middle of a busy office, with the phone ringing and no voicemail available, then the following six-second exercise will help prepare you to take the call:

> > > E X E R C I S E < < <

- Place both feet on the ground, stand up straight and grow as tall as you can. Stretching your body like this automatically gives you more confidence.

- Take a deep breath, tilt your head back and look at the ceiling.

- Place a pencil or pen horizontally between your teeth, hold onto both ends and push it back as far as you can (there is no need to bite the pencil). This has the effect of stretching your facial muscles around your jaw and mouth, causing them to lose their rigidity. As your face relaxes, your voice will too.

- Count to three, take the pen or pencil out of your mouth and then answer the call with a belief that you are going to resolve any problem right now.

We all have those occasions when we have to take a call at a difficult moment, or when we do not have the right answer for the caller, but use this little exercise and you will soon be feeling much calmer about any such conversation.

This is something that is particularly relevant in relation to call centres, information centres and helplines taking reports of problems.

If we are not careful, as callers, we can find ourselves getting so frustrated at speaking to someone with a strong accent we find difficult to understand that we end up experiencing 'telephone rage' (see next section).

It is very easy to misunderstand people over the telephone; see below for an example of how this happened to me:

• • •CASE STUDY• • •

It was Christmas Eve and I had been invited to a party in Wallington, just outside London. I wanted to make sure that I could get back from this party on public transport, so I phoned the rail enquiries line for advice.

I was shocked to find that there were trains only once an hour and that the fare was five times what I had expected.

I struggled to understand the enquiry line staff member when he repeated my destination, and it turned out that he thought I wanted to leave from Warrington, which is about 200 miles away in the northwest of England.

For you to avoid similar experiences and to help you really listen to what is being said, use open body language. The exercise on the following page will help you with this:

- This works whether you are sitting down or standing.

- Relax, take a deep breath and expand your lungs. Place both feet on the ground and adopt natural breathing, with palms open and, where possible, facing the ceiling.

- Breathe in, lower your shoulders and imagine that there is a string pulling your shoulders together behind you. The more open you are, the easier it is to assimilate information. When you hear something that contradicts your perceptions, first verify what you heard, then ask some questions until you understand the situation. Remain in this position to get information over the phone successfully, even in difficult situations.

Telephone rage

As a pragmatist or extrovert there are three things to remember when you answer the telephone to someone who is angry and stressed – be receptive, apologetic and calm your desire to 'win'. On the other hand if you are an amiable or analytical personality your natural response is to go into defence mode when someone is ranting and raving.

For all personality types, remain calm and make sure you listen to what is being said to ensure you get to the desired outcome for both parties – a mutually beneficial solution to the problem.

The first skill you need to acquire is matching the flow of the other person's voice – the speed of their speech and the pattern of their pauses – so that you are both on an even footing. Gradually bring the speed of the conversation down (and the pitch, if the other person has a raised voice) so the whole conversation becomes calmer.

Another great tip is to stand up. If you are like most people the first movement you do when answering the phone is take a seat. We have done two exercises now that demonstrate that you sound clearer and more authoritative if you are sitting up straight. However, if you are speaking with someone who is in the midst of 'telephone rage', then it is even easier for you to appear influential when you are standing up as the energy is allowed freedom to flow unchecked.

When we are under pressure in a telephone conversation, our body language skills can end up completely forgotten, which will be evident in our voice. It is vitally important when speaking to someone who is angry that we keep in control of our own breathing and posture so we can turn the conversation around.

Dress for success

Although working from home may seem a relaxed way to go about business, it is even more important for those who do so to adopt a professional attitude while speaking to clients on the telephone.

You may think that when the person you are speaking to is not able to see you, they have no idea of how you are dressed. This is not the case! If you try to do business in your pyjamas, without having a shower and with unwashed hair, then you will come across to others as sloppy and lacking in concentration during your conversations with them.

Preparations for working at home should be exactly the same as if you were going to the office that day. When you dress for success your mind and body prepare to do business. So put the suit on, comb your hair and slick on the lipstick.

Be disciplined because if you look and dress like a professional then this is what will come across on the telephone. The other person can tell if there has been no effort to present yourself professionally, as it comes across in your voice and attitude and you will be caught out.

• • • C A S E   S T U D Y • • •

The owner of an IT company phoned one of his homeworkers, a member of his customer support team, at the start of his shift at 9am one morning. Having spoken to him for about five minutes, the owner asked him if he was still wearing his pyjamas and eating his breakfast. 'Yes!' came the startled reply from his homeworker. 'How did you guess?'

'Well,' replied the boss, 'your telephone manner was not as sharp as it should have been and you sounded a little hesitant and distracted. You didn't sound as if you were entirely in work mode. I therefore surmised that, given the time of day and the fact that you are at home, you were not yet dressed for work, and as you were distracted the likelihood was that you hadn't finished your breakfast.'

Never be tempted to multitask

Often when we are talking on the telephone, we start looking at and doing things unrelated to the conversation we are having: we multitask.

This is no way to do business and will be obvious to the person at the other end of the phone. It is very tempting, particularly for extroverts and pragmatists – especially those who are baby boomers and think they have good telephone skills – to try to send an email at the same time as having a phone conversation, as we believe the other person won't know and we can cross two things off our to-do list at once.

As we can only form a relationship with someone on the telephone based on their tone of voice and the words they are saying, it is vital that during any such conversation the only thing that the two people involved are focusing on is the discussion they are having.

As well as being tempted by tasks on your to-do list, other sounds in the room can also be distracting when you are on the telephone.

The two main faculties that you use on a telephone are hearing and speech. Your hearing is something that is available all the time you are awake; there is little that you will not hear that is taking place nearby. Of course, you are able to select what you hear, and if you are experienced at meditating you will be able to distance yourself from what is happening around you to concentrate on your own tasks, but generally background noise can be very distracting when you are trying to have a telephone conversation.

Carrying out the exercise below before you make your telephone call will help you to block out sounds around you to focus on the conversation in hand.

> > > E X E R C I S E < < <

- Close your eyes and place your cupped hands over your ears. Let all other thoughts apart from the conversation you need to have just drift away.

- Hold this pose until you feel calm, then slowly take your hands away from your ears. You will now hear what is really close to you much more clearly, and your focus can move to that telephone conversation where you will only hear what is being said.

Below are the key telephone skills you should now be aware of:

- Make sure you smile when on the telephone, as this will reflect in your voice.
- People judge you by their perception of authority.
- When we take deep breaths we relax and can then concentrate on the task in hand.
- It is very easy to misunderstand people over the telephone – make sure you really listen to what is being said.
- It is even easier for you to appear influential when you are standing up.
- When you dress for success your mind and body prepare to do business.
- It is vital that people speaking on the telephone focus only on the conversation in hand.

CHAPTER THREE

Email, text and social networking

CHAPTER THREE
Email, text and social networking

Having lost both visual communication and tone, all we can work with now is the words we use, a circumstance that can compound the breakdown of communication. This chapter will look at how to communicate effectively through email, text and social networking.

Emails and text messages

Text messages and emails have revolutionised communication as we can now message people instantly, no matter where they are in the world. This is an area that is relatively new to businesses, having arisen within the last 30 years or so, and therefore is something that generations X and Y are said to be most proficient at. However, there are some pitfalls all generations should be watching out for when using email and text messaging.

It makes us lazy

When using text and email we don't need to think about having a conversation. In fact it is becoming more popular to replace words with icons and symbols, such as smiley faces, to portray how we are feeling. While these can be helpful as a replacement for the tone of our voice, it is causing people to limit their vocabularies.

It is also easy to think that because the recipient of your email doesn't know what you are wearing, what you are doing at the time or even where you are that you aren't giving out an impression. Beware – you are! While it may not be as extreme as the recipient being able to tell that you are still in your pyjamas, as with the telephone example earlier in the book, if you don't check your email carefully then you may find that you make spelling errors or miss words out, suggesting to the recipient that you aren't giving the communication with them the care it deserves.

Now, a word of advice to extroverts, like myself, who are always in a hurry to get onto the next task – make sure you re-read your message to avoid mistakes like this occurring.

The case study below demonstrates just how important it is to check your emails carefully before sending them.

••• C A S E   S T U D Y •••

A client I work with was once reprimanded by her boss for sending an email out to their marketing database with a spelling mistake in the subject line.

While it may only seem like a small error to make, it gave the impression of the company being sloppy (particularly as they were trying to tender for marketing contracts) and therefore was damaging to the company's reputation.

When you are communicating with someone, whatever method you are using, then that person deserves your full attention.

Emails can be misconstrued

Your intended meaning when writing an email and the recipient's interpretation of it could be completely different.

The case study over the page llustrates how many interpretations there can be of something very simple:

Some months ago I was running a workshop about communication and used the simple statement 'the cat sat on the mat' to demonstrate to the class how much our interpretations can differ.

I asked each of the participants to imagine a cat and a mat and then tell us all what colour they were. In a group of 30, every cat and every mat was completely different. Try this with your friends and see what happens.

What we perceive is based on our previous experiences and own personal journeys, and therefore it is likely that you could carry out this exercise an indefinite number of times and never find another person who pictures the same cat and mat as you do.

Equally, if you send an email to someone believing the tone and content say one thing, they may interpret it completely differently. The example below shows how dangerous this can be:

In August 2009 the New Zealand Herald reported on the case of an Auckland-based accountant who lost her job after sending an email which contained bold type and capital letters in order to emphasise a point.

The accountant had reportedly caused 'disharmony in the workplace by using block capitals, bold typeface and red text in her emails' and therefore she lost her job as a result.

While losing your job may be an extreme punishment, this case study demonstrates why you should always re-read your emails to make sure they aren't going to be misconstrued. If content proposed for an email or text message is sensitive, it is always best to discuss it on the telephone or, ideally, face to face.

Emails and text messages are impersonal

You can't use your tone of voice or body language to soften anything you say in an email or text message, and when used alone words can appear very harsh. The case study below demonstrates this:

• • • C A S E   S T U D Y • • •

In May 2003, *The Inquirer* reported that over 2000 people learnt that they had lost their jobs when British Amulet Group sent a text message to them. Part of the message read 'you are being made redundant with immediate effect'. It does seem rather impersonal and not what we expect of HR departments these days, and one wonders how the people felt as a result of this action.

It was later revealed that text messages were used so that all staff members received the message at the same time. However, making the tone of the message more sympathetic would have softened the blow considerably. Pragmatists are particularly bad at adding 'social niceties' to their messages. I would surmise in fact that the person at British Amulet Group who sent the message is probably a pragmatist!

It is important to remember that while email or text messaging can be a quick way to convey information, and can even be something to hide behind if the message you need to deliver isn't very nice, people deserve respect and if possible these forms of communication should be avoided for conveying sensitive information.

The tone and body language skills you have learnt in this book should now equip you to better deliver unpleasant information face to face.

Take care over the language you use

It is important when sending an email or text message to use non-threatening words to validate your point. You need to remain composed, open and fair, as you are unable to enhance your message with your body language. Here are some simple ways of helping you achieve your aims while using language that is less likely to cause upset.

Remove any mention of 'you' and 'I' in all written communications as it seems less accusing. If this is unavoidable ensure at the very least you replace 'you' with 'I' so the responsibility lies with you, not the recipient. Compare the following three sentences:

'You have made a mistake on this advert, and you will need to correct it before I can sign this off.'	This is harsh and accusing, and is likely to cause the recipient to be defensive and unresponsive.
'There are a few alterations that need to be made to this advert before I can sign it off.'	This is better, and places the responsibility on your shoulders, but still sounds a little accusing as you are telling the recipient they have left you unable to do something.
'Great ad! It works really well! We just need to make a few more tweaks and then we can sign it off.'	This reads as if nobody is at fault, the advert is simply just not quite finished yet. We have also used some encouraging and praising vocabulary.

Social networking

Social networking is a relatively new phenomenon favoured by Generation Y, who have been brought up with the internet and the new opportunities it presents. But, as with emails and text messages, there should be some caution used when communicating through social networking.

Social networking allows you to create a false personality

Even though the social networking sites are slowly introducing the visual aspect back into communications through the use of photos and avatars, it is very easy for people to fool others into thinking they are someone they are not by using images that aren't of themselves.

People can use social networking sites to hide their insecurities and build a picture of someone they would like to be; however, this is a dangerous trap to fall into. It is impossible to keep up this pretence and in the end you are bound to trip up. If you are leaving false information on different sites no one can build a true impression of you and what you stand for.

It is always better to be honest and open at all times – that way others can interact with you and help you become the person you would like to be.

Online vs. reality

People can get so engrossed in their online profiles that they end up forgetting who they really are. If we aren't careful, we end up with more of a life online than face to face with others. The example over the page shows a very extreme example of this:

In March 2010 the *Daily Telegraph* reported on a story about a couple who neglected their real-life daughter in favour of caring for an avatar daughter on an online lifestyle game. The pair spent several hours roleplaying caring for their online baby in internet cafes, leaving their baby daughter home alone.

The length of time they spent with their virtual baby gradually increased until they were regularly spending 12 hours at a time with the internet child. One evening they returned home to find their real-life daughter had died while they were gone. It was later discovered that she died from prolonged malnutrition. A police officer working on the case said at the time, 'They indulged themselves in the online game of raising a virtual character so as to escape from reality, which led to the death of their real baby.'

While there are very few people in the world who will take their virtual world so seriously that it has a profound effect on their real world, this example does demonstrate a need for caution when using social media.

Today's Generation Y businesspeople are in danger of being so distracted by generating blog posts, Tweets and Facebook statuses that they may neglect to pick up the telephone and have a one-to-one conversation with their clients and colleagues. While social media are excellent for attracting new clients and leaving quick messages for friends, they should never be a substitute for direct conversations.

- Make sure your emails don't contain spelling mistakes or miss out words, which makes you look sloppy.
- If you send an email to someone in the belief that the tone and content say one thing, bear in mind they may interpret it completely differently.
- When used alone, words can appear very harsh.
- It is important when sending an email to use non-threatening words to validate your point.
- Remove any mention of 'you' and 'I' where possible in written communications as it seems less accusing.
- While social media are excellent for attracting new clients and leaving quick messages for friends, they should never be a substitute for direct conversations.

CHAPTER FOUR

Webcasts and YouTube

Webcasts and YouTube are another phenomenon that is growing quickly. As human beings we have a desire to see the person we are communicating with, which is why video is becoming so successful. If we are unable to see the person we are talking to we build a picture of them in our mind, which can turn out to be completely wrong when we do finally meet them.

How often have you built up a relationship with someone over the telephone, only to meet them in person some time later and find they are nothing like you imagined them to be? The advent of webcasts and videos means we can now see the people we are communicating with, bringing all three elements of body language back into play.

An amateur video with poor body language may be OK for family and friends (though you should be demonstrating good body language at all times to help it become a habit), but in the business world the presentation of ourselves is vital for success. Many companies now prefer videos to paper CVs when recruiting people, while businesses are using web videos to demonstrate their expertise – in both cases your body language needs to be perfect.

As webcasts and promotional videos aren't filmed live, you can do much more advanced preparation with your body language before filming. There are five key areas you should consider.

Posture

When filming your video, you must appear straight and tall on screen. By raising yourself up you will look relaxed and confident, giving you more credibility. There are four exercises you should carry out to ensure your body language is saying the right things about you.

1. Making an entrance

It is important to be noticed, and how you make your entrance is the first chance to do so. On walking into a video podcast, a restaurant, your boss' office, or onto a stage, you should be aware of your posture.

Stand tall with the head erect and the shoulders back; pause and survey your surroundings then walk slowly forwards. To perfect this walk, practise in front of a mirror, keeping your eyes in contact with the mirror as you walk towards it. Keeping upright, walk smoothly and slowly – do not forget to pause and look around you. Keep practising until you feel comfortable and it comes naturally.

To most people it is alien to walk slowly; we tend to walk quickly in a hurried gait, head down, looking as if we are panic stricken with no time to spare. When we walk slowly with our head held high others will notice us. Try this out for a week in different situations and I guarantee you will get noticed.

Once mastered, this exercise will come easily when required. It is OK to speed up again and rush around like a headless chicken when necessary but remember to keep coming back to this stance so that you remain focused and calm when trying to impress.

2. The tail exercise

Once you have mastered walking slowly and steadily, the next step is to keep your spine straight. To do this you need to imagine a long tail growing from the base of your spine. What does this do to your posture?

You should find that the imaginary tail strengthens and straightens your spine keeping your body upright.

3. The cape exercise

The next step is to open your body in order to appear approachable and reliable. This can be achieved by imagining you are wearing a cape on your shoulders. As soon as you put the cape on you will find your shoulders pull back to balance your imaginary cape, leaving your body open and relaxed.

With the cape on your shoulders you can become whatever you wish – you are proud, you are regal, you are fearless. Placing the cape around you will give an instant lift to the spirits. If you are feeling nervous prior to an on-screen interview, simply take a few steps around the room with the imaginary cape on your shoulders, the nervousness will disappear and you will become confident and ready for anything. It really does work wonders.

4. The crown exercise

Once you have mastered your slow and steady walk, as well as moving across the room with your cape on, the final step is to add your crown. Place an imaginary crown onto your head and see what a difference it makes to your posture. You can no longer stoop forwards or slump your shoulders because your crown would fall off. The crown will keep your head straight and facing forward, while the cape will keep you open and approachable.

Now that you have made your entrance and attracted the attention of the viewer, you need to ensure that you stand still when talking to them. Having a person moving about on screen is very distracting and makes it much harder to focus on what they're saying; therefore it is equally important to appear balanced when on screen. The exercise below will help you stay balanced while presenting:

> > > E X E R C I S E < < <

Standing Still

To stand still without moving you need to place both feet firmly on the ground, legs together, arms at the side. It is best done in bare feet but wear low-heeled shoes if necessary. Feel the three balancing points of the feet – at the base of the heel, under the big toe pad and the area above the small toe. Look straight ahead to a point in front of you and relax into this pose.

After a few minutes, be aware of any movement – are you swaying slightly, and to which side? Do you tend to lean forwards or backwards? What do your hands want to do?

Return to the original pose and carry on for another five minutes, keeping the feet still. How do the bases of your feet feel – are they steady and firm, and do you feel balanced? Are the calf muscles tense or are they relaxed, holding you steady?

Over time, you will find that your body aligns, the spine straightens, the head is erect and the mind is still. This is actually a Hatha yoga pose called 'The Tree', which some of you will already be familiar with.

If you are sitting down in your video then it is your hips that will control your balance. The maintenance of good posture with no slouching shows that you are not a pushover and that you are standing in your own power, so you should make sure that you are sitting with your feet flat on the floor and your spine straight in the chair.

As with the previous exercises, imagine you are wearing a cape and crown to make sure your shoulders and head are balanced and centred.

Where are your arms and hands?

Using your arms indicates passion, and as long as you are doing it naturally, your hands can be very influential. Politicians such as Tony Blair and Barack Obama are very good at using their hands to persuade listeners to accept their way of thinking. They very often use a technique called 'steeple hands', which sees their hands placed together with the tips of the fingers and thumbs meeting whilst the heel of the hand is pulling towards the elbow.

There are various versions of this in which the shape is implied but the fingers do not touch, or in which the hands point upwards or forwards. To present your case, use the hands pointing up in a 'steeple' gesture, and then have your hands pointing towards the person you are communicating with when you are listening to them.

This 'steeple' body language signal is a behaviour that brings confidence. Master the use of this and you will be taken more seriously. Using both hands while talking will always give other people a clearer idea of what you are saying.

On average our arms are two and a half times the size of our face, so can look very large and distorted on screen. Make sure you keep them out of focus as much as possible – you should use them for emphasis only!

Breathing

Before you record your podcast or web video, it is a good idea to practise your breathing. I recommend an advanced yoga breathing technique called circular breathing.

> > > E X E R C I S E < < <

While sitting down, take a breath in through your nose or mouth and then exhale without a pause. While breathing, imagine the air as a white mist circling inside you. Breathing in this way helps you to become focused and calm and ready to take on new challenges.

You will need to practise this breathing exercise a few times to perfect the technique before you use it for your live production – don't start it just before you record something live! Because the exercise stops the pauses between the breaths you may find that you feel a little dizzy after a while, so don't do it for very long – just three or four minutes per session.

Tone

It is important to ensure that your tone of voice is relevant to your audience. Tone and inflection of the voice affect the message and our body language simultaneously, so the message we are giving out will be different for each person and in different situations.

Your voice and posture must suit your audience in order to influence, therefore sometimes it is sensible to walk away from doing a web video if you don't have the right voice for it. If we want to record a training session for our website, for example, then we will need a modular voice, one of honesty and truth, so the audience listens and takes part. Sports commentators, who are generally excited when presenting, would be the wrong type of person for a sensual hair advert!

You should also take advantage of the fact that you can re-record your web videos; never use the first video run you film. Watch it and adapt it until you have the right inflection in your voice and right posture in your body for your marketplace.

Do not underestimate how much your body language will change with your voice presentation. For example, if you start shouting it becomes very hard to move slowly – have a go now and see for yourself! Equally, if you are walking very slowly it's very hard to talk quickly. It's best to work out the characteristics you want to present and then think about how you can get your voice to embody them.

- When filming your video you must appear straight and tall on screen.
- When we walk slowly with our head held high others will notice us.
- Having a person moving about on screen is very distracting and makes it much harder to focus on what they're saying.
- If you are sitting down in your video then it is your hips that will control your balance.
- The 'steeple' body language signal is a behaviour that brings confidence.
- On average, our arms are two and a half times the size of our face, so can look very large and distorted on screen.
- It is important to ensure that your tone of voice is relevant to your audience.
- Sometimes it is sensible to walk away from doing a web video if you don't have the right voice for it.
- You should take advantage of the fact that you can re-record your web videos; never use the first video run you film.
- It's best to work out the characteristics you want to present and then think about how you can get your voice to portray them.

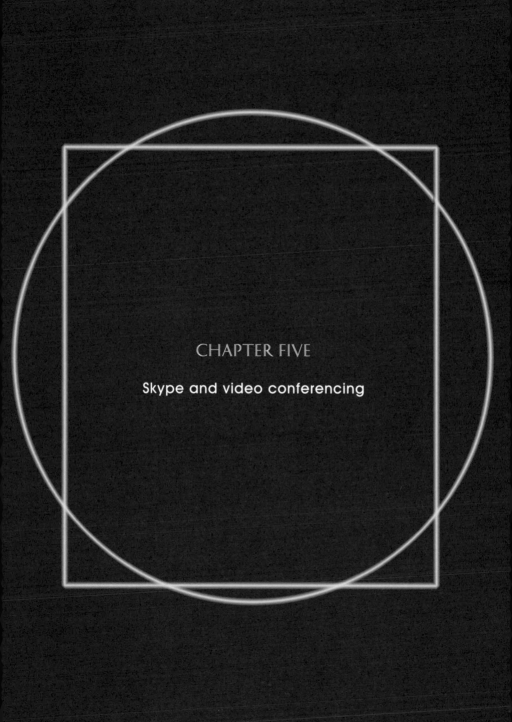

CHAPTER FIVE

Skype and video conferencing

With Skype or video conferencing you are performing live, so it is vital that you are giving a good impression and getting it right first time. In this chapter we will equip you with some techniques to deal with the pressures of a live performance.

Skype is an online communication program that uses Voice over Internet Protocol (VoIP) for voice communications and instant messaging (IM) for chat. If both parties have webcams, you can add in a visual aspect as well, meaning that all three aspects of body language come back into play.

Video conferencing gives two or more people the ability to interact over the telephone through voice and video in real time. Video conferencing was born of a need for people to communicate with others face to face and re-introduce the visual element to conversations.

The pressure of being live

To be on show at all times can be tough. In this situation all four personality types and all the different generations are outside their comfort zone. There is no escape if you have not combed your hair or put your make-up on when the caller comes online. Also, because you are live, and can be seen, you are much more exposed so you need to ensure you go into the conference or call grounded, centred and prepared.

Without your feet firmly on the floor you will fall over in a negotiation. A strong stance will give you a much better chance of being seen and heard. Any movement or shuffling of feet allows your audience to lose concentration on what you are saying; the stiller you are, the more you command.

If you are not comfortable with who you are right now, and are nervous about a call you are about to go into, then try the following grounding exercise.

This is also a great exercise to try in the morning if you feel tired, even if you haven't got a big call or meeting coming up!

- Jump up in the air as high as you can and land on two feet. Now start walking and feel how much more balanced and grounded you are with additional energy.

- Don't forget to remove your shoes first if you are wearing heels or heavy shoes.

Don't forget you're on camera

Even when you are able to see other people through their webcam, it can be easy to forget that they can see you through yours, so I strongly recommend that you re-read the visual body language section in Chapter 1 to brush up on your skills.

Skype in particular can be very dangerous as users, including myself, are so busy sending files and chatting with text and voice that there is no time to look at the other person while communicating. It is much more likely that you will be relaxed and using different body postures to the ones you would use if you could see the other person in front of you.

The case study over the page demonstrates a conversation that I took part in on Skype, which was completely ruined by the person I was speaking to forgetting that he was on camera and using inappropriate body language behaviour:

About a month ago I had a Skype call with a salesperson in the United States who was seated at his office desk, with all his certificates behind him. Within minutes, this immaculately dressed man stretched his arm outside the frame of my camera and spilt his coffee all over his desk. The next thing I knew, I was looking at the top of his head while he mopped it up. He was still talking during this process, but it was so funny and distracting that it was really not a good use of my time, so I rebooked the call with the top of his head.

Now, I am sympathetic to accidents, but this was such a poor display of body language skills. Firstly, he had positioned himself behind his desk, giving him a position of power. I would rather work in collaboration, and that means removing barriers between us, such as the desk.

Secondly, he was so preoccupied by his coffee and by having too much on his desk, that he clearly hadn't prepared properly for our meeting by creating a professional environment.

The situation was exacerbated by the fact it was a Skype call and all I could see was the top of his head as he cleaned up his spilt coffee.

It is important to remember that any movements made by you on screen are really noticeable to the other person and could distract them from the conversation. Whether using Skype or video conferencing, you now have the option of seeing yourself on screen at the same time. I recommend always having this option turned on as a reminder of how you present yourself.

It is not easy to look away when all your conversation partner sees is a talking head just inches from their eyes. Remember the last time you had a conversation this way – how much notice could you take of anything else around you? This new focus on the head necessitates some new skills, without which there is a risk of giving out unintended information, some of which are outlined below.

Raising eyebrows

This can indicate that you are either dismissive of what is being said or that you are inquisitive and need to know more. If you are having a conversation with someone who raises their eyebrows you will need to establish which of these is the case. You can do this very easily by asking open questions to establish their needs.

Head protruding forward

This can look very aggressive so if your head naturally protrudes forward you need to make a conscious effort to use open body language to avoid looking unapproachable. If you are talking to someone whose head is protruding forward tread gently with them as they may be feeling frustrated.

Fast blinking

This indicates that you are trying to process information quickly or that you are very nervous. If you are working with someone who is blinking a lot try slowing the conversation down to help them.

Placing your hands over your face or mouth

This is an indication of someone needing reassurance or feeling stressed under pressure. Avoid placing your hands over your mouth when speaking on Skype as it also makes your words harder to hear.

Make eye contact

It is tempting to look at the screen when talking on Skype, as that is where the other person's face is. However, you actually need to make sure you are looking into the camera in order to be looking directly at them. If you make the mistake of looking at the screen then your conversation partner will be looking at your eyelids rather than directly into your eyes.

Interaction is key

When taking part in a video conference, it is important to interact with everyone else – make plenty of eye contact with the other participants and acknowledge their presence.

In his book *Body Language: How to Read Others' Thoughts by Their Gestures* Allan Pease states that when we are watching someone presenting, 87% of our communication with them is carried out via the eyes, noting posture, eyes and feet, if they can be seen, 9% via the ears and 4% via other methods such as intuition and tone of voice.

This means we should be paying particular attention to these areas when presenting to someone using video conferencing technology.

Eyes

As so much of the communication of our message is achieved through eye contact with the recipient, it is vital that our eyes look bright, alert and focused. There is nothing like sparkling eyes to help you look attractive and there is a quick, cheap and practical way to achieve this.

> > > E X E R C I S E < < <

- Get a large, luminous highlighter pen and hold it with an extended arm in front of your nose. Pull your hand in close to your nose, while keeping your eyes fixed on the pen at all times.

- Do this repeatedly for a minute or two with each arm and your eyes look and feel refreshed.

Another tip for when you are on screen is to use a pencil to get your viewers to follow movements or look at information on screen. While doing this be sure to be talking about what is on screen and not anything else, so as not to distract the viewer.

Ears

Ears move very little in body language terms; they may go red for some people when they are angry, or others may touch them when they are thinking or sometimes even lying. But in this context it is more about listening than the ears themselves. It may seem like a very small percentage, but we are still conveying 9% of a message by what the recipient hears us saying, so make sure the words you use are helpful to them.

There is more information about using appropriate vocabulary on page 38. You should also make an effort to make sure that you listen more than you talk. As the old saying goes, you were given one mouth and two ears, so use appropriately.

Other methods

If you can see the feet of the person you are talking to then that could give you clues as to how they are receiving your message. When we point our feet in a certain direction we are pointing to where we want to go.

To appear open in a video you need to open your feet out, placing them firmly on the floor to make a slight 'v' pattern, with your heels pointing to each other and the toes out. Make sure your head and feet are in alignment when you are on video or delivering a presentation.

Intuition is also important when talking with someone on Skype or on video. Intuition refers to the ability to understand what someone is saying or thinking without having to use any effort and, as our forms of communication speed up, this is something you will really need to develop.

We are born intuitive: we know who our mothers are and who is going to be good to us, and if we don't like people then we cry. As we get older we bin intuition in favour of logic! However, it never quite leaves us, and this quick exercise will demonstrate this to you:

> > > E X E R C I S E < < <

- Sit back to back with a partner or colleague, with both feet flat on the floor. Relax and breathe normally. One of you needs to choose three topics and say them out loud to your partner. In your mind you must choose one of these topics, but don't reveal which one.

- Give this a go for three minutes and see if you have both picked the same topic. Then swap over and let your partner have a try.

- When I did this with a class of 18, only one couple did not achieve the right result. The closer you can sit back to back the better

Be prepared

Although it is easy to position yourself in front of the camera so that only your face is visible, it is important to present yourself in a professional manner.

A report by Chicago University found that when we are interviewing or presenting to someone, the recipient makes up their mind about us within just seven seconds. This means it is vital that we make a great first impression.

What we wear and how we hold ourselves show in our body language and in the energy we are subtly giving out to the other person. So, dress for success! You will feel that you are in business mode and will be prepared to talk online in a businesslike manner.

Prior to going online and starting your business day, it would help to prepare yourself by aligning your body to sit in comfort. Slouching is bad for your posture and also looks unprofessional if an unexpected Skype call comes online! Try the exercise below to help align your body for the day ahead:

> > > E X E R C I S E < < <

- Stand up and lean your body to the left hand side. Jump in the air and when you land with both feet on the ground, notice how your spine has straightened and you are now standing up straight.

- Repeat the exercise on the right side of your body and you will see it has the same effect.

It is also helpful to practise breathing exercises before starting a video or Skype call. A great exercise that I use regularly is to breathe in slowly, holding the breath for a few seconds, and breathe out slowly to a count of five. Do this three or four times and see how it leaves your mind clear and your face alert and gets you ready to begin the day.

You need to make sure that you are relaxed before you appear on screen. A great way to do this is to focus on relaxing your whole body one stage at a time. Begin by concentrating on your tongue and making sure it is really relaxed in your mouth. Then move your attention to your eyes and jaw – you will notice your face begins to soften and relax. Now soften your toes and hands as this will ease any tension in your limbs. If you are holding your tummy taut, soften that too. Stay in this relaxed position as you start your video call.

Managing multiple conversations

It is possible to run several online conversations at a time on Skype, which is great if you are very busy and need to communicate with several people at once, or if you want to bring more people into the conversation.

However, I do have a word of warning. It is easy to get conversations mixed up, so proceed with caution if you are talking to lots of people at once!

• • • C A S E   S T U D Y • • •

I was talking to two business contacts overseas, in their time zone (the middle of the night in the UK), when I saw a message from my boyfriend pop up on screen. I immediately read his message and then went back to one of my business colleagues to answer a question he had asked.

I then switched again to what I thought was my boyfriend's link and answered his question. I then had a sudden realisation that I had just posted the message to my boyfriend on the business contact's link – all very embarrassing.

So, when talking to several people at once and switching quickly between different conversations, be sure to let people know that you are dealing with more than one conversation early on, as it allows for time lapses and just might make it easier if, like me, you get mixed up once in a while.

An even better solution is to avoid multiple conversations if at all possible and focus on the task in hand to be sure to achieve the results you want online.

- With Skype or video conferences you are performing live so it is vital that you are giving a good impression and getting it right first time.
- Any movement or shuffling of feet allows your audience to lose concentration on what you are saying.
- It is easy to forget that people can see you through your webcam, just as you are able to see them.
- When taking part in a video conference it is important to interact with everyone else – make plenty of eye contact with the other participants and acknowledge their presence.
- What we wear and how we hold ourselves shows in our body language.
- Proceed with caution if having multiple conversations on Skype so you don't mix them up.
- An even better solution is to avoid multiple conversations if at all possible and focus on the task in hand to be sure to achieve the results you want online.

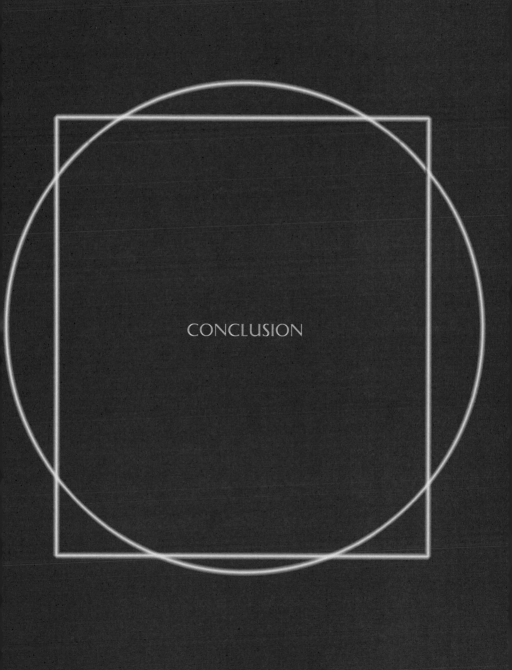

CONCLUSION

CONCLUSION

In the introduction to the book we looked at how each generation has learnt different skills as they have used technology through their lives. This book has shown that all three generations need to brush up on their skills in order to excel at communication in the future. Here are some tips for each generation as it goes forward:

Baby boomers (born between 1946 and 1964)

These people are great with face-to-face communication (though of course it is never good to become complacent, so I would always recommend reading the face-to-face section to ensure your skills are up to date!). However, as businesses are using social networking and multimedia more and more, I would strongly recommend you become comfortable with the skills discussed in chapters 4 and 5.

Although some of the face-to-face skills will be familiar to you, it is important to be aware that there are some significant differences between on-screen and face-to-face meetings.

Generation X (born between 1965 and 1981)

Members of this generation have great telephone and instant messaging skills, so will be able to handle many of the skills needed for Skype calls and video conferencing, but I would like to suggest that you read Chapter 1 to help you develop your face-to-face skills.

It will also be helpful to spend some time on the social media section in Chapter 4, so that you are ready for any changes in technology that may happen over the next few years.

It is widely believed that you have the upper hand when it comes to technology and its fast-changing ways, but it is important to brush up on your face-to-face skills too – so I would like to point you to Chapter 1. In July 2010, Clay Shirky, a professor at New York University's Interactive Telecommunications Program, told *New Scientist* magazine that 'we thought we'd all end up as video heads in the virtual world interacting in some great big virtual-reality console, but here's the big surprise: there are almost no long-lived online-only communities. When a community is online for long enough, those people start arranging to meet up in the real world'. This shows that, although you may be excelling in video and social media skills, if you don't brush up on your face-to-face body language you may be left behind when the invitation to meet up arrives on your doormat.

We also introduced the four different personality types. As with the different generations, there are some key points that each personality type can take from reading this book.

Pragmatist

You are characterised by your ability to complete tasks quickly. Your movements are quick and direct and you are particularly frustrated by people who take too long to respond or give you what you need. While these are great traits to have, as it means you are organised and efficient, you can sometimes forget to add the 'social niceties' when sending emails or messages. I would suggest that you pay attention to the exercises that help you remember this as you will find people respond to you much better!

As you are very task-led, you can also be tempted into multitasking, especially when having a telephone conversation and you think the person on the other end doesn't know what you're up to! What you are doing will leak into your voice and you will be caught out, so make sure you slow down and structure your day so you are able to give your full attention to people when talking to them.

Finally, I would advise you to pay attention to your voice. Pragmatists tend to use their voices to dominate and you would benefit from talking more gently to allow others to be heard.

Extrovert

As with pragmatists, you tend to do everything at a fast pace and are very task-led. This means you also need to be careful not to multitask while on the telephone. It is important in all communications to give the other person your full attention, even if you think they might not notice when you aren't.

If you find yourself dealing with someone who is angry, whether in person or on the telephone, then you will also need to calm your desire to 'win' the conversation. Extroverts tend to get very agitated with people and want to achieve the upper hand in conversations, but this is not the best way to solve the problem. If you find yourself doing this then try some of the calming exercises in the book and make sure that you are acting in the best way possible to achieve the best results from the conversation.

Finally, a word of warning when sending emails: extroverts are characterised by their trait to do things in a hurry, so take time to re-read emails to ensure there are no mistakes in there!

Analytical

Analytic personalities are naturally closed when it comes to body language, so you will need to make a conscious effort to use open body language signals so people can communicate with you easily. To do this you should keep your palms facing upwards, which indicates that you are open to conversations, and have your legs and arms uncrossed to encourage people to approach you.

Another thing to bear in mind is that as an analyst your natural response to conflict is to become defensive and avoid the situation. If faced with someone ranting and raving, this is not the best way to solve the situation. Instead you would be better to remain calm and use your natural skills to ask open questions to come to a resolution.

Amiable

Amiable people are characterised by their need to please people, so you will avoid saying no or doing anything that could cause conflict. As such, you are naturally shy about looking people in the eye for fear of being intrusive. However, to really communicate with someone effectively this is a valuable skill to learn. Practise the exercise on page 29 in Chapter 1 until you become more comfortable with this.

As with analytical personalities, your natural response to conflict is also to become defensive and avoid the situation. My advice to you would be the same: remain calm and ask open questions in order to come to a resolution.

Thinking for a moment about where body language is heading next, it is my belief that we are going to be interacting in person less and less as technology takes over. Therefore when we do meet face to face, it needs to be very professional.

I believe that in the future we will find that large gatherings will take over from small face-to-face meetings. The world seems to be moving faster and we feel the need to interact with more people at once to save time (this is already evident in the fact that Skype and videoconferencing with many people at once is already replacing one-to-one meetings in the work place).

Over the next few years I think we will find ourselves speaking to hundreds of people at a time, delivering seminars and workshops to many clients simultaneously. Our body language will need to adapt to allow for this.

It is also my belief that we will find that we interact with technology much more than we do face to face even if the person is in the room with us. It is already possible for our Blackberries to 'shake hands' to share our details with someone we meet at a networking event, so gone are the days of handing out business cards and talking to someone about what we do.

Looking forward, I think this will go one step further, with our details being held in a chip in our clothing or shoes, so we will know all about a person without even needing to speak to them. Our body language will have to adapt to make the best of this technology and new behaviours will develop.

It is important to stay abreast of these changes so that we don't get left behind.

'The world is moving so fast these days that the man who says it can't be done is generally interrupted by someone doing it.'
Elbert Hubbard, American author and philosopher

WHAT PEOPLE SAY ABOUT
CAROLE RAILTON

'Carole is a lively and proactive person who infects others with her enthusiasm and ideas. Very passionate about what she believes in, she has the rare talent of listening well while others put their views across. She practises what she preaches and it is always possible to glean some really useful pearls of wisdom and perspective from her during any conversation. Creative, confident and caring – an excellent mix of attributes!'
Steve Westall, Co-director of Pansophix

'I found Carole Railton's book to be full of self-improvement exercises designed exceptionally well to help find out what makes us tick, as well as finding out what sets us apart. Carole helps to unlock the true potential of the reader in manageable bite-sized exercises that help you grow as a person. The book for me was a voyage of self-discovery.'
Andrew Cuthbert, CEO of Omnisoft Services

'Carole is an inspiration! Full of life and ideas, and a voice of calculated reason and calm in today's hectic world. Carole's innovative techniques and fascinating ideas provide an everyday formula for strategic personal success.'
Will Broom, CEO and founder of London Launch Ltd

'As long as I have known Carole, which is no small time, she has been dedicated to understanding how people do what they do and how to influence. So it came as no surprise to me to learn she has written this book on body language. As always it will no doubt convey her usual passion and infectious enthusiasm for the subject.'
Keith Francis, President of Peak Force Limited

'I've worked with Carole several times over the years and she is one knowledgeable lady! Her face- and body-reading skills are super-impressive and super-insightful. Carole can read people like a book. And now she has a book. Perfect.'

Bibi Lynch, Journalist and Broadcaster

'Since meeting Carole and reading her book, I have been amazed at how much better my communications are. She has brilliantly made me much more aware of the power of non-verbal messages. As a result, I present better, understand when to adapt my body language and do some of her techniques before working with new technology so as to have the greatest impact. This book is essential, not just for those seeking to improve their business communications, but for everyone, as it will help them all.'

Moira Taylor, Consultant Events Manager and Editor